How to get a distinction at A

Introduction

The fact that you are reading this, means that you are serious about getting a distinction in your next ABRSM exam. By *putting into practice* the advice in this e-book, you can be confident of doing just that. As a teacher of the ABRSM syllabus for over 30 years, I can pass on to you, the benefit of my experience, which has enabled my own private students, to obtain results, well above the national average. Since 2009, the ABRSM has stopped publishing their statistics, but the last available ones, show that only 50% of students taking exams, got a merit or distinction. At the time of publishing this e-book, I have entered over 200 students for ABRSM exams since 2005 of which, 78% got a merit or distinction in the last year. *So your in good hands.*

Getting a good mark, is not just a question of spending hours and hours of practising your instrument, but knowing *how* to practice and also knowing *what the examiner is looking for.* As well as studying the official ABRSM marking criteria, I have done in depth analysis of the comment sheets that are given to the students with their results, which are very revealing in this regard.

In the following pages I have broken down the four aspects of the exam; Scales, Pieces, Aural and Sight Reading and you need to give adequate attention to *each* of these aspects in order to get a distinction. So are you ready to start preparing for your next exam and get the mark you deserve? Then read on.....

<u>Sight Reading</u>

It is no coincidence that this aspect, is the first one I want to mention. So many times I have heard, "I can't sight read", and in a recent poll I took on my YouTube channel, most people said it was the hardest part of the exam. The result is, that many of the same people, put sight reading "on the shelf", maybe opening a specimen sight reading book a week or two before the exam and then they are "surprised" to find they are poor at sight reading.

A couple of weeks before your exam is too late.

If that is you, ask yourself the question,

"Is it logical that you spend the least time working on your weakest aspect?"

Surely you would want to be spending ***more*** time on those parts which you cannot manage so well.

However, mindlessly ploughing through pages of specimen sight reading books is unlikely to produce a good mark in the exam.

You need to know what the examiner is looking for. Most students' approach to sight reading, is to struggle through note by note, without any attention to fluency or rhythm. In the ABRSM's official marking criteria for a distinction, ***the first thing that is mentioned is "Fluent, rhythmically accurate".***

So why are so many students who take exams so bad at sight reading fluently? Here's the usual scenario. You practise the same three pieces for the exam, over and over for many weeks, maybe months, to a point where you have virtually memorised them and so, you are really doing very little reading of music.

Sight reading music, is no different to reading normal English text. When you were in your first year of school, you couldn't read fluently, but with years of practice, you can now read a previously unseen English text, as if you were speaking normally, fluently and with feeling and emotion. *Music is no different*. So the first key to sight reading success, (maybe too obvious to say, but so many don't do it,) is to practise it regularly.

Another reason, linked to the above, why many cannot read fluently is because they have gotten into a habit of looking at their hands (if you're a pianist). The fact that you have memorised your 3 pieces, means you have the luxury of being able to look at your hands. I often observe students who perform, what I like to call, "vertical tennis", when playing a new piece. Look at the music, then look down at their hands to play the note they have just worked out. Then look up again, for the next note, down again, up again etc. etc. Hardly likely to produce a fluid performance.

Here is my prescription for breaking this habit. Start with something *very easy.* Try to sight read something from a book you used many years ago. *Set a metronome to a slow pulse*, say 60bpm. Before even placing your hands on the instrument, clap the rhythm of the melody in time with the metronome.

Then place your hands in the correct position and continue to play the passage *without looking at your hands* and keeping in time with the metronome.

As you get used to playing without looking at your hands, your fluency will improve and you can move on to increasingly more difficult passages.

Now, I know that this advice applies more to pianists, but in my experience, pianists tend to have more problems in playing *fluently* than other instrumentalists, exactly because of this "visual distraction." However, whatever your instrument, clapping the rhythm or at least hearing the rhythm in your head, before trying to play the notes, is essential for fluency.

Furthermore, playing the correct notes fluently, with the correct rhythm is not enough for a distinction and this e-book is about how to get a *distinction* in an ABRSM exam. For the very top marks, the examiner will also be looking out for your attention to musical detail. This includes dynamics and articulation. In the exam, you are given a 30 second preparation time before the test and according to the official syllabus notes, you are free to try out the passage in this 30 seconds. This is where many students go wrong. They *waste* this preparation time, struggling through the first few notes of the test and when that time is up, they have probably not looked much past the first bar.

This is my second prescription for successful sight reading. Using the same principle as above, find an easy piece which you will play against the metronome as described earlier. However, before you start the test, give yourself 30 seconds in which you should do the following:

For the early grades (1 and 2) in piano, *just find the first note* of each hand, notice the finger that is suggested to put on that note which will give you, your hand position. Then noting the key signature, just play a five finger run, (a micro scale) using the notes that are under the hand position you have just found. (In these early grades, all sight reading tests will be in one closed hand position). So for example, if you were given a starting note of E with 3rd finger and a key signature of F sharp, play the five finger run, C, D, E, F sharp, G. This will give you a sense of the key you are in.

For other grades and instruments, look first at the key signature and then play a one octave scale of that key. All sight reading tests for any grade or instrument will only use the notes and range that correspond to the scale requirements of that grade.

Be careful to identify whether the key is major or minor. Minor keys are usually obvious by the presence of extra accidentals and you should incorporate any of these in your initial scale or five finger run (micro scale).

All of this should take just a few seconds. Next, ***don't start playing the piece,*** instead scan ahead for any musical details such as dynamics, or staccato/legato markings. Don't just look at them, but try to ***imagine how it will sound, building a mental picture*** of the musical shape of the test.

Then scan for the highest and lowest notes of the test and any large intervals between the notes. By the way, up until now, you have not played a single note and your 30 seconds is almost up. Don't panic - you have used your preparation time wisely.

Finally, in any remaining seconds of your preparation, choose what seems, at first glance the most challenging part of the test and practise this, ***not necessarily from the beginning.*** Then after 30 seconds, put the metronome on and perform the test, without stopping or correcting any mistakes.

Speaking of which, a word on mistakes....

If you ***do*** make a mistake in a sight reading test, ***do NOT*** go back and correct it. You will be, in effect, making TWO mistakes, because you have now, also spoiled your rhythm by going back and correcting it.

With this in mind I have prepared on YouTube, a series of Sight Reading Tests where the notes disappear, just before you are about to play them. You can find them easily on the homepage of the YouTube channel MusicOnline UK

Using this playlist ensures that you;

1. Read ahead - a technique you use when reading normal text in order to read fluently and
2. Are prevented from going back in an attempt to correct any mistakes.
3. You keep in time, since these videos require you to play along with a pre-recorded track.

You should also know some basic Italian terms, especially those related to tempo, which may be used in the tests to indicate how they should be played.

Attention to such musical details is necessary for a distinction and even to get a merit, the official ABRSM marking criteria cites, "adequate tempo" as a requirement. So *know your Italian terms.*

As you go through the grades, the complexity will increase in the music you are required to play, so make sure you are familiar with all the following elements depending on your grade and instrument.

Grade 1
- 2/4, 4/4 and 3/4 time
- Simple dynamics
- Simple note values
- Simple articulation
- Occasional accidentals (within minor keys only)

Grade 2
- Dotted notes
- Tied notes

Grade 3
- 3/8 time
- Two note chords in either hand (for pianists)

Grade 4
- 6/8 time
- Starting on an up-beat (anacrusis)
- Chromatic notes
- Pause signs and tenuto markings

Grade 5
- Simple syncopation
- Ritardando
- 4 part chords - maximum of 2 in each hand (for pianists)

Grade 6
- 9/8, 5/8 and 5/4 time
- Triplet rhythms
- Changes of clef
- Use of right pedal (for pianists)

Grade 7
- 7/8 and 7/4 time
- Changes of tempo
- 8va sign

- Use of *una corda* (for pianists)

Grade 8

- 12/8 time
- Simple ornaments
- Three note chords in either hand and spread chords (for pianists)

Finally, I want to draw your attention to another criteria for a distinction, mentioned in the official ABRSM mark scheme. To give you the best possible mark the examiner will be looking for

"Confident Presentation".

Think of the test as a ***musical performance.*** It is not just a test on if you can recognise basic pitches and rhythms. Try to play with conviction. Now you might say, "that's easier said than done, if I'm struggling with the notes", but if you practice sight reading ***enough***, in the way I have described above, there should be no struggling with the notes and you can still play confidently with conviction and musicality, ***even if you do make a slip or two.***

Aural Tests

The next section of the exam I am going to discuss, is the aural tests. These are often, like sight reading, one of the most feared parts of the exam and again, like sight reading, for the same reason, left until the last minute before the exam. Fear, comes from a lack of confidence and confidence in itself, comes from a lack of preparation.

It is worth noting, that in the official ABRSM marking criteria, to get a distinction, the examiner is looking for **confident responses,** whereas the description for a pass below merit includes the phrase **cautious responses.** I often tell my students that even if they are not sure about the answer to a test, "sound like you **are** sure". This has on occasions been evident in the mark sheets given after the exams, where regularly an examiner has noted that the student answered confidently - **so they are looking out for this.**

Secondly it is worth noting that it is always worth having a go - even if you haven't got a clue. You get 6-8 marks for just having a go. Zero is only awarded if you don't even try. (This rather strangely means that marks 1-5 don't exist).

The next big hurdle to confidence is simply shyness when singing. Unless you are a singer most of us may be a little embarrassed to sing in front of others, especially if the range goes a little high. Start off practising at home, just singing simple phrases increasing the pitch range of these gradually. Again, on my YouTube channel you will find the "E Aural Trainer" which can help you build your confidence in this regard.

Remember too, that pitch rather than vocal quality is important. I would recommend starting any note with a consonant sound such as lah, dah, or tah. You could hum the answer, but singing with an open mouth to a note with a definite beginning like "dah" is more likely to be in tune and this will help your confidence. Humming is more likely to produce a "shy, inward" response. Remember, the examiner is looking for this *confident response*.

Support your note with your diaphragm (the muscle you feel contracting when you cough). Feel this muscle contracting as you sing, maybe placing your hand below your belly button at first, to help sense this support. This too will give you more confidence on the day.

The examiner should adapt to your vocal range and you could even hum or whistle the responses to the "sung parts of the test" - however singing is probably more suitable to most.

Finally be prepared - know what to expect. The tests follow a very precise formula. If you know what the question will be, even before it is asked, this will help you feel more prepared. There is plenty of practice examples on the E Aural Trainer playlist on my YouTube channel that I mentioned above, but in addition, on the following pages you will find some grade specific hints and tips so that you know exactly what to expect:

Grade 1

A - Clapping the beat and recognising two time or three time.

Be careful to clap the beat and not the rhythm of the test you hear. Also be aware that, if you seem to be clapping very fast, you may be clapping the quavers within a beat, rather than the beat itself. Another mistake is to start clapping too early. The syllabus states that you should join in as soon as you can, but this may cause you to panic before you have had enough time to feel the beat. If you come in after a couple of bars, when you have had enough time to assess where the strong beat is, then that is adequate enough to fit the description "as soon as you can". As far as ***stressing the strong beat*** is concerned, a whole hand clap could be used on the first beats of the bar and a two finger clap could be used on the other beat(s).

B - Singing back phrases.

In addition to using a consonant sound like "dah" and supporting your note with the diaphragm, be aware that the three phrases you need to sing back will be exactly two bars each. You are supposed to respond ***in time.*** That means that as soon as the examiner has played two bars, you start singing on the next beat. This is made somewhat easier by the fact that he will count in two bars, i.e. The same as the length of the first phrase that is to be played.

C - Recognising a change in pitch.

This test is made easier by knowing that only one note will change and all you need to do is identify whether the change was at the beginning or the end.

D - Questions on Dynamics and Articulation
In this test, there will be **two** questions. One will be about the dynamics. Note that the question may be about whether the changes in dynamics were sudden or gradual. The second question will be about articulation, that is, whether the playing was smooth or detached.

Grade 2
A lot of the tests in Grade 2, are very similar to those in Grade 1.

A - Clapping the beat and recognising two time or three time.
See Grade 1 above.

B - Singing back phrases.
See Grade 1 above. Note however the range of notes will increase slightly from three notes to five, so be prepared to sing possibly a little higher.

C - Recognising a change in pitch **or** rhythm.
This again is similar to Grade 1 above, but now you will need to say not only **where** the change occurred but also **how.** Typical answers to this question could be, "there was a change in rhythm at the beginning" or "there was a lower note at the end".

D - Musical features
In addition to the dynamics and articulation from Grade 1, (this will be one of the questions), the second question will be about tempo. A typical question will be, "Did the speed of the music change anywhere or did it always stay the same?" Notice the word **anywhere** invites you to state **where** the change was. Also, if there

was a change, it will be a *gradual* slowing down or speeding up. Don't just answer, "it was slower at the end", but rather, "it *got* slower at the end".

Grade 3
A - Clapping the beat and recognising how many beats in a bar.
In addition to what was required in Grades 1 & 2, you will also need to distinguish between 2 time and 4 time. This can be a little trickier, but as with other time signatures, try to feel how often a strong beat occurs, if the 1st and 3rd beats are *equally* weighted it's 2 time, if the 3rd is a little weaker, it's 4 time.

B - Singing back phrases.
As Grades 1 & 2 above. Again the range of notes will increase to a range of an octave, maybe singing some octave scales will help here.

C - Recognising a change in pitch or rhythm.
Exactly the same as Grade 2, except the phrases get longer and could also be in a minor key (which shouldn't really add any extra difficulty).

D - Musical features
There will be two questions. One question will be about the topics covered in the above grades, dynamics, articulation or tempo changes and the second question will be about tonality, that is, is the piece in a major or minor key. This generally gives students very little problem, major sounds happy, minor sounds sad.

Grade 4

A - Singing back a phrase.

In this grade the phrases get longer and therefore harder to remember, so they are played twice before you need to sing them back. Before the test, the examiner gives you the key chord and starting note. It might be a good idea to hum this starting note before he starts playing the test and see if you can still hum this starting note after the first playing and before the second.

B - Sight Singing

Although one of the most daunting parts of the aural tests, this is one you can practice easily on your own. Play a C major chord and then the note C. Then try to sing random notes that are no further than a third away from this C, (that is A, B, C, D or E) checking each note by playing them on your instrument. Most students find singing down a step or third harder than singing up, from the previous note, so make sure to practice this especially.

C(i) - Musical Features.

As with other grades, this is accumulative, in that the first question will be about features you have already practised in Grades 1-3 above. The second question will be about the character of the piece. A typical question will be something like, "What musical features, give this piece its character?" Notice that there are two parts to this question. First you need to mention a musical feature, which could be the tempo, the articulation, the tonality and *then* say what mood it creates. So a model answer could be something like, "The slow tempo in a minor key makes this piece sad". ***Prepare a few set answers that cover the basic moods before the exam.*** E.g. Happy, Sad, Lively, Calm.

C(ii) - Clapping a rhythm and identifying how many beats in a bar. Although it is a separate test, this is classed as part (ii) of the C test and herein lies a little trick. You will need to clap the rhythm and state the time signature of a short extract from the *same piece* that was used for C(i). Now if you have already worked out your answer to the character of the piece, before the examiner has finished playing it, you can already be thinking about the time signature, way before he asks the question. In fact you will have heard parts of this piece *three times* before he even asks about the time signature, ample opportunity to prepare your answer.

NOTE - You only need to say how many beats in a bar, not say the time signature as such.

Grade 5

A - Singing back a phrase.
No real change from Grade 4 above, except phrases might be longer.

B - Sight Singing
Again, this test is very similar to that of Grade 4B above. There will be 6 notes to sing instead of 5 and also the interval of the rising 4th to the tonic, will also be required. To practise this, like above, play a C major chord and the tonic note C. Then try to sing the 4th below it (G) and back to the tonic. Also the notes may go up to a fifth above the tonic, but never more than a third away from the previous note. So when you are testing yourself you could try a pattern like; C, E, D, F, E, G, but there will be no need to go from C - F or G for example, or D - G.

C(i) - Musical Features.

As with other grades, this is accumulative, in that the 1st question will be about features you have already practised in Grades 1-4 above. The 2nd question will be about the *style and period.* The periods you need to be familiar with are, *Baroque, Classical, Romantic and Modern/Contemporary* (previously one could say 20th century, but now music written since 2000 is coming into the aural tests). Here are some of the main features of the different periods, which will help you identify from which one a given extract comes:

Baroque music was very elaborate, often with many ornaments, the melodies would be difficult to sing or memorise and the harmony was created by individual voices conversing with each other - known as polyphonic harmony. Because baroque music was originally for the harpsichord and not the piano, the dynamic range is not as great as in later periods and also the keyboard was shorter - very high or very low notes were not possible. Regarding dynamics these tended to be terraced, that is crescendos and decrescendos were not used, rather there were more sudden changes.

Classical music on the other hand was much more refined and simple, the melodies could be easily remembered and sung and the harmonies were generally made by a tune with simple accompaniment - know as homophonic harmony. Phrases were clearly defined and regular. The idea of crescendo and diminuendo also came into use during the classical period.

In the **Romantic** period, melodies were still singable and easily memorable, but the intensity of emotion was much greater. Harmonies became richer, texture thicker and dynamic range much wider. Tempo was much freer and the use of the sustain pedal was now very prevalent in this period.

Modern music (20th/ 21st Century music) is easily recognised by its discordant use of harmony. That said, 20th century music also includes jazz and impressionism, the latter being the style of composers such as Debussy in which the music often has a blurry misty feel giving an "impression" of something rather than a dramatic picture of that thing.

C(ii) - Clapping a rhythm and identifying how many beats in a bar. The same as Grade 4 above, but the phrases may be longer.

Grade 6
A - Singing the upper part
This should really be no more difficult than Grade 5, only this time the melody will be accompanied by a lower second part. Initially this can be off putting but with practice you should be able to hone into the top part. As in previous grades, the examiner will start the test by playing a key chord *and the starting note.*
If you hum this starting note to yourself, before the test and see if you can repeat it before the test is played the second time (you'll get it twice), this should help train yourself to concentrate on the upper part.

B - Sight Singing with accompaniment.

This is of course, quite a step up from singing in free time without an accompaniment as you did in previous grades. You will need to think about rhythm as well as pitch. What might first seem off putting (the accompaniment), can actually work in your favour. There may be common notes between your part and what the examiner will play, or there may be imitation, so a figure played in the accompaniment might be echoed in your part a bar later. In the test you will get about 15 seconds preparation time. Use this time wisely. Like sight reading on your instrument, don't just start at the beginning and work out the first few notes. Scan ahead, look for the things mentioned above. Look for awkward intervals. Also try to have a sense of key. Does it finish on the tonic? (You'll get a key chord to start). Although one of the hardest parts for most students, this skill can be improved with practice.

C - Identifying a perfect or imperfect cadence.

After one of the hardest parts, comes what is probably the easiest part of the Aural Tests for this grade. The two chords at the end of a phrase make what is called a cadence. If the phrase sounds finished, like the piece could end there, it is a ***perfect cadence.*** If it sounds unfinished, like it could go on further, it is an ***imperfect cadence.*** Another way to recognise a perfect cadence is that it ends on the tonic triad or key chord. This key chord will be played at the beginning of the test, so if the last chord of the phrase is the same as the chord played at the start before the test, then the cadence is perfect. This test is made even more simple, by the fact that the examiner will play it twice, although from my experience, most students can answer it on the first playing.

D(i) - Musical Features.

As with other grades, this is accumulative, in that one of the questions may be about features you have already practised in Grades 1-5 above. The other question will be about **texture and/or structure.** It is also possible that **both** questions might be about texture and structure (i.e. one about texture, the other about structure).

Texture is the way the different parts interact with each other horizontally. Think of it as the layers of a sandwich. Some possible textures might be;

- A single melody line.
- Tune and accompaniment where a melody is supported by chords.
- Homophonic (literally one sound), similar to tune and accompaniment but in particular here, there is no rhythmic independence between the parts, they work together rhythmically as one sound.
- Polyphonic (literally many sounds) also know as contrapuntal, where the different voices act independently, maybe in a "question and answer" manner, imitating or echoing each other. In this case it would be extra impressive if you could identify how many voices you can hear.

Structure on the other hand is how the phrases are related vertically. Typically, the short tests that you get in the Aural section of the exam might have two or three sections. Are these sections related? If for example, the first and last sections are the same or very similar, with a contrasting middle, it is called **ternary form** (ABA), whereas if there are just two main sections quite different from each other it is called **binary form** (AB).

D(ii) - Clapping a rhythm and identifying how many beats in a bar.
See C(ii) Grade 4/5 above, but the phrases may be longer.

Grade 7
A - Singing the Lower Part.
This test is similar to what you had to do at Grade 6 level, except now you need to sing the lower of two parts. As before, the examiner will play the starting note and it will help you "tune in" to the lower part, if you hum this quietly to yourself after the examiner plays it. Also you can practise on your own trying to hear and sing the lower note of some random two note chords played on a piano.

B - Sight Singing the Upper Part of a two part phrase.
Again, similar to Grade 6, only now you will have not a chordal accompaniment, but a single line "second voice" against what you need to sing and this is likely to be more rhythmically independent from your part. However, it is quite probable that there will be some imitation, so in your preparation time, scan ahead for any clues that might help you.

C(i) - Identifying cadences.
In addition to the perfect and imperfect cadences you were required to recognise at Grade 6, now there may also be **interrupted cadences.** This shouldn't be any harder as the interrupted cadence is easy to identify, in that it goes into the opposite tonality to that of the piece. That is, if the piece is in a major key, it will end on a minor chord and vice versa.
Another way to recognise an interrupted cadence is, it sounds like it was going to finish with a perfect cadence, but then on the last

chord it takes a sudden change of direction, it gets *interrupted.*

C(ii) - Identifying the chords that make the cadence.
Connected to the last test, you will need to identify the chords that made the previous cadence. Here a little theory knowledge is useful.
- A perfect cadence is always V - I.
- An interrupted cadence is always V - VI.
- An imperfect cadence will always end with V, but the previous chord could be I, II or IV. In this case you will need to listen very carefully to the bass line. All chords you need for this grade are in root position, so you simply need to identify the degree of the scale of the penultimate note as the 1st, 2nd or 4th which should be quite easy because the examiner will play the key chord, just before playing the two chords that make the cadence.

C(iii) - Identify a modulation.
A modulation is when a piece of music changes key, by adding an accidental that is not normally part of the key signature. The options for this test will be modulations to the *dominant, subdominant or relative minor.* The last of these three is the easiest to recognise. It is a little bit like recognising an interrupted cadence in that there is a tonality change from major to minor. A modulation to the dominant, involves *adding a sharp (or losing a flat),* giving the harmony a *lifting feel.* The opposite is true for a modulation to the subdominant. In this case, a *flat is added or a sharp is lost* giving the harmony a *sinking feeling.*
Be careful not to confuse these lifting or sinking feelings, with rises and falls in the melody which could, for example, be

descending as the harmony rises by an accidental occurring that is raised from what is in the key signature.

D(i) - Musical Features.
There is nothing new in Grade 7 that is not covered in Grades 1-6 above. Questions can be on any of the topics already covered, i.e. Dynamics, articulation, tempo, tonality, **character, style/period, texture or structure.** However they are more likely to be about the latter topics in **bold** above.

D(ii) - Clapping the rhythm and identifying the beat.
This is very similar to the test C(ii) Grades 4/5 or D(ii) Grade 6, except now, you will also need to distinguish between two time, three time, four time *or 6/8 time*. As you should know from your theory, 6/8 time subdivides the beat into triplet quavers, so listen out for these three shorter divisions within each beat.

Grade 8
A(i) - Singing the lower part of a three part phrase.
This is very similar to test A at Grade 7, except that now there will be three parts not two, yours being the lowest. That means that there will be a little more going on to "distract you", but if you follow the advice given above for Grade 7, you will be well prepared.

A(ii) - Identifying a cadence.
The list of possible cadences that could be used now includes, perfect, imperfect, interrupted *or plagal.* The first three were covered in Grades 6 and 7 above, so the only new one is the plagal cadence (IV-I). This is sometimes called the *"Amen"*

cadence on account of it being used to close many phrases used in church music. It can be recognised by the fact that the **tonic note** is used in BOTH the last two chords. (The examiner will play the tonic triad/key-chord before the first playing of the test, which is played twice). For example, in the key of C major, the plagal cadence will be the chords F major and C major. Play these two chords while, at the same time, singing the tonic note C to the syllables *"A-men"* and you'll see what I mean. So, if you can hear the tonic note in both the last two chords, then the cadence is plagal. Like the perfect cadence, because it finishes on the tonic triad, it feels "finished", but the ending is softer, not so *final* as in a perfect cadence.

A(iii) - Identifying three chords of a cadential progression.
In this test, the examiner will next play the last three chords of the phrase used in test A(ii) and some theory knowledge will be useful, i.e. knowing the following progressions:
- Perfect cadence   V - I.
- Imperfect cadence I, II or IV - I.
- Interrupted cadence V - VI.
- Plagal cadence IV - I.

However, you will also need to listen very carefully to the bass line, because from this you need to work out the possible inversions of the above chords. They may include any of the following: I, Ib, Ic, II, IIb, IV, V, Vb, Vc or VI.
Additionally, the dominant (chord V) might be a dominant 7th (but only in root position), which has a richer sound than the plain dominant.

What will also be useful is to know the tonality of the different chords. For example, if you have recognised that the bass note of a chord is the 4th degree of the scale, then the chord could be either IIb or IV. Now for a piece in a major key, chord II is minor whereas chord IV is major. Similarly, in a minor key piece, chord II is actually a diminished chord, and chord IV is a minor chord. Try to get used to these different *colours* of the chords to help you identify them using a combination of a) theory knowledge b)hearing the bass note and c) the tonality or colour of the chord.

B - Sight Singing a lower part.
Building on the skills you have mastered in earlier grades, you now need to sing a *lower* part. The advice given above, still applies regarding looking for clues, imitation and common notes from the accompanying part. You can additionally practice this yourself by singing a melody and playing on your instrument the same melody at an interval of a third above. For example, you could sing C, D, E and simultaneously play E, F, G. This is probably easiest on a piano or other instrument that does NOT require your breath, but playing chords is also possible on wind instruments at an advanced level by playing one note and singing the other - a great exercise for tuning your ear.

C - Identifying modulations.
Similar to test C(iii) in Grade 7 above, where a modulation could be to the dominant, subdominant or relative minor, but now there is an additional option of a modulation to the *relative major.* That means that the key of the piece could start in a minor key. (In Grade 7 all the modulation tests started in a major key). For major key tests there will be NO difference to what was required for

Grade 7. This will be the first question you will get in the exam.

The second question *will start in a minor key.*
- If it ends in a major key, the modulation could have been either to the relative major or the dominant major.
- If it ends in a minor key, the modulation could have been to the subdominant or the dominant minor.

Now although you do NOT need to distinguish between the major/minor variants of a modulation to the dominant in the exam, the two options for each final tonality can create some confusion. So for this you will need to listen carefully to the bass note of the final chord. (The examiner will play a key chord before the test). Also a modulation to the dominant has a much stronger feel. Try these examples to get used to the sound of each:
C minor-D major-G major = Modulation to dominant major
C minor-D major-G minor = Modulation to dominant minor
C minor-C major-F minor = Modulation to subdominant
C minor-B flat major-E flat major = Modulation to relative major

D - Musical features.
Like all the grades above you should listen out for Dynamics, articulation, tempo, tonality, **character, style/period, texture or structure** concentrating on the last four in **bold**. The extra difficulty in this grade is that the examiner will *not* ask you specific questions, only a very general question such as, "comment on any notable features in this piece". This requires you to be more *creative, more aware,* listening out for anything you could comment on. You can do this with every piece of music you come across, whether listening or performing, trying to

identify in particular the **character, style/period, texture or structure.**

Conclusion

The above hints and tips are all very well in theory, but to be confident of getting a distinction, you need to prepare this section of the exam with lots of listening experience. For this purpose, there are many practice and training videos on my YouTube channel as well as extra Premium content on the website www.music-online.org.uk. A simple Google search for **E Aural Trainer** will point you in the right direction, helping you to become familiar with what will be expected and so this in turn will boost your feeling of confidence on the day.

<u>Scales</u>

Many students find learning scales rather tedious and as such may neglect preparing them well for an ABRSM exam. However, they are possibly one of the easiest parts of the exam to get full marks in. In fact it was ONLY in the scales section of the exam, that I always got full marks, many years ago as a teenager.

I would recommend *starting* your practice with scales, it not only gets them out of the way, if they are not your favourite thing to practise, (a bit like eating your least favourite vegetable first on your dinner plate), but also it acts as a good warm-up for your pieces. I would also recommend *starting your exam with scales*, (you get a choice), for the same reasons.

Of paramount importance is fingering. Take time to learn your fingerings accurately. Many students have said to me in the past,

"Does fingering matter? I played all the correct notes."

Yes it *does* matter. It is true, in the ABRSM regulations, it states that "Candidates are free to use any fingering that produces a successful musical outcome". However, "any fingering" does not refer to a random fingering that just "happens" on the day. Sometimes I have suggested alternative fingerings to the ones written in the ABRSM scale books. What *is* important, is that you use *the same fingering* every time you play a particular scale.

In order to play scales securely, you need to develop muscle memory, so that your fingers "automatically know where they are going". Muscle memory is only developed by repeating the same action over and over again, and this in turn can only be achieved if you use the same finger pattern every time. By the time you get to the higher grades, the scales will be going so fast *you need to be on autopilot*, you won't have time to think!! Here are a few tricks to help you remember the fingerings of major scales

C, G, D, A and E majors.
You're probably aware that these follow a basic "3 - 4 - 3" finger pattern and when you came across the first three in Grade 1, you probably had little problem learning these. One of the greatest challenges for students between Grades 1 and 2, is putting these scales hands together. However, it helps to notice, that "3's are always together", so if you are using a third finger in one hand, you should be doing the same in the other hand, at the same time. Then, I like to liken the hands together scales, to a couple dancing, where the man leads. On the way up, the right hand is the man, that is to say, that it will do the changes of "3 - 4 - 3" just before the left hand and on the way down, the roles are reversed where the left hand *leads* the 3 - 4 - 3 pattern.

B flat, E flat, A flat and D flat majors.
These all follow one pattern.
● RH ascending and the LH descending for *all* these scales, the thumb always goes after the black note or group of black notes if there are more than one consecutively.
● The RH descending always puts 4th on B flat, and the LH

ascending, always uses 4th for the first cross over.

F major, B major and F sharp major.

To be honest, B major and F sharp major (and also D flat major, but this has already been covered above) despite their many sharps (or flats in the case of D flat major), are some of the easiest scales, because there are only certain places where the thumb *can* go and that's where you put it. Regarding the finger that crosses over onto the black notes, I like to think of the black notes as "***big group/small group***". Obviously, a big group will need more fingers, so when approaching a big group you cross over your 4th finger. Likewise when approaching a small group you cross over your 3rd finger.

Interestingly, in all three of these scales (or four if you include D flat major), thumbs are always together in both hands, except for the very first and last note in the case of F major.

About speed:

You will lose marks if you play your scales too slow. However, you will also lose marks if you play your scales so fast that they become untidy. Again, the ABRSM regulations state that they should be played "at a pace that is consistent with accuracy and distinctness". The higher grades will require you to play your scales at a faster pace. On the next page is a table of the recommended speeds for the various grades at ABRSM piano.

Grade	1	2	3	4	5	6	7	8
Scales (including contrary motion, chromatic and whole tone)	In twos @60 bpm	In twos @66 bpm	In twos @80 bpm	In fours @52 bpm	In fours @63 bpm	In fours @76 bpm	In fours @80 bpm	In fours @88 bpm
Arpeggios (including broken chords, dominant and diminished 7ths)	In 3's @46 bpm	In twos @63 bpm	In twos @69 bpm	In twos @76 bpm	In twos @88 bpm	In fours @50 bpm	In fours @56 bpm	In fours @66 bpm
Scales in 3rds						In fours @52 bpm	In fours @46 bpm	In fours @52 bpm
Scales a 3rd apart							In fours @60 bpm	In fours @63 bpm
Scales in 6ths/a 6th apart							In fours @52 bpm	In fours @63 bpm
Chromatic scales a minor 3rd apart								In fours @76 bpm
Chromatic scale in minor 3rds								In fours @52 bpm

Notice how the notes are grouped. For example in Grades 1-3 above, you play two notes to a beat, for the basic similar motion scales, in Grades 4-8, four notes to a beat. However, referring once again to the syllabus, it states that they should be played ***"Without undue accentuation".***

Consider for a moment the scale of B major on the piano. It so happens, that the fingering pattern has the thumbs always together and thumbs can sometimes **bump** or play heavier, so that you could end up with an accent on every thumb note (i.e. on the B's and E's).

If you think in fours, with a very slight lean on the first note of every group of four, you will put the emphasis on a different note, i.e. B, F sharp, C sharp, G sharp, D sharp, A sharp, E and finally B again, thus creating a more even tone throughout the scale. It is also a very good way of counting octaves. Sometimes at the higher grades when playing four octave scales, one can lose count of how many octaves one has played. If you think in groups of four, using the example of B major again, you will arrive on the tonic B as the first note of a group of four, ***as you finish the fourth octave.***

Now, although, much of the advice given above is very *piano specific"* grouping notes in fours, is good advice for any instrument as there will always be tendencies to give undue accentuation to certain notes within a scale, and playing them in fours will counteract this.

Another point worth considering, to give yourself the best chance in the exam, is to mix up the order you play your scales. If you always play them in the same order, when the examiner asks you for a random scale on the day, this might put you off.

With this in mind I have prepared some flashcards, again on my site www.music-online.org.uk/p/scales.html which will randomise the list each time and then you have the option to play again the ones you got wrong. Incidentally, the same web page has links to a video demonstration of every scale you will ever need for an ABRSM or Trinity College piano exam.

Alternatively you could make your own scale cards, that is, little pieces of card with the names of each of the scales written on them. Then you place them in a pot and pick one at random. If you play it well, place it in a different pile of "correct" scales. If you play it wrong, don't play it again now, put it back in the pot and try a different scale. It will come up again later and you want to practise getting it right first time, not 2nd, 3rd or 4th time in the exam. This will also ensure, that the scales you have the most difficulty with, will get the most practice.

Continue like this until the entire pot, has been transferred to the "correct" scales pile. And then the next day start again.
Finally, don't forget to practice them hands separately, as the syllabus requires "hands together *or* separately", even if you are on a higher grade. You may be surprised to know, how many of my students can play very well a scale hands together, but if I ask them to do a single hand, it completely confuses them. It's like their muscle memory has adapted to *"hands together only"* and the autopilot is totally confused when there is a change to the

norm. Think of a plane that is designed to fly on two engines, but could safely manage on one in an emergency. Some adjustment would be necessary and pilots would be trained and practised in what to due in such situations.

Be prepared, for all possible variations in the exam. The same is true for staccato and legato variations in the higher grades. Admittedly, the list of scales in the higher grades is quite long, so you could alternate **"*staccato / legato*"**, but the next time you practice, start the other way around, i.e. **"*legato / staccato*"** so that every scale gets equal amounts of practice with both articulations.

Pieces

In order to get a good mark on your pieces in ABRSM exam, it is not just a question of playing the right notes with the correct rhythm. It is probably good enough to pass at lower grades, but as you go up to the higher grades, there must also be a sense of involvement when playing, communicating the mood and style to the listener.

With this in mind, getting a good mark in an ABRSM exam starts right back with *choosing* your pieces. You should listen to the all the options and then choose the one that inspires you. You will play a piece you enjoy the most, better. When my students pick their pieces, I start by playing them the three options in the list. I then ask, "Which one did you like the best?"

Sometimes they will respond something like, "The first one looked the easiest", to which I will point out that they are all as difficult as each other, only sometimes, to the less trained eye, the *hidden* difficulties may not be so apparent.

The next step, is *not* to start learning the notes, but to *listen* to other *good performances* of the piece. Makes notes on how others interpreted the piece, the shaping, phrasing, dynamics etc. You are a musician, an artist, NOT a technician.

YouTube has become a very popular resource for students to learn their exam pieces. However, there are a lot of ***very poor quality performances*** on the platform, particularly for pianists.

What compounds the problem, is that if you search on YouTube for a particular piece, invariably what comes up first in search, is a certain channel that has been around the longest and so has the most subscribers and hence, views. Being first in search, doesn't make it the best.

You will NOT get a distinction by copying the performances of Alan Chan.

... Indeed many of his performances, particularly at the higher grades, would barely scrape a pass, let alone get a distinction. If you do use YouTube, try to find performances that you find ***musically engaging***.

To get a distinction in your pieces, a good place to look, would be at the official ABRSM marking criteria. The assessment is divided in 5 parts:

1. Pitch
2. Time
3. Tone
4. Shape
5. Performance

So lets take a look at these individually.

Pitch

This one is quite self explanatory. For a distinction, the examiner will be looking for ***"highly accurate notes and intonation"***. (Intonation, is only in the case of instruments where the performer has some control over the tuning of the instrument, so not so relevant to pianists.)

To be accurate in pitch, you need to have built up a good muscle memory. If there are particular technical difficulties, start practising slowly, maybe with a metronome. If you are stumbling on a particular passage, you are playing it too fast. It is ***always better to play slowly without mistakes*** than fast with mistakes. Remember, in music, ***a hesitation is a mistake.*** Don't try to run before you can walk. You'll find slow methodical practice, ***gradually*** increasing the speed, will develop muscle memory, so that you eventually will be able to play fast, effortlessly. On the other hand, if you approach it too quickly at the beginning and are always making the same mistake, you are then reinforcing the habit of making that mistake.

Metronome practice, while invaluable for learning technically difficult passages, does have its downside. It can make your playing sound very mechanical and unmusical. Once you think you have learned the piece technically, ***put the metronome away.***

Be careful though, sometimes we tend to memorise pieces to such a point, that we don't even look at the music and this can be a recipe for developing bad habits, even playing wrong notes without even noticing. ***Always practice from the music.***

When I say "practice" from the music. I don't mean, I am against playing from memory. In fact, I did all my exams from memory and got a distinction in every one. At the end of your ***practice,*** by all means, give a ***performance*** without the music.

A useful exercise might be, (after you *think* you have learned a piece,) to take a small section each day and play it extremely slowly, (even if you can play it at four times the speed), observing every note, its length, its articulation, its fingering, dynamic level. Then repeat the small section a few times, gradually letting the tempo return to normal, but still being aware of all the minor details you noticed before. Playing a piece over and over from beginning to end from memory *is not practising.*

The expression goes, "the devil is in the detail".
I would suggest to you, *"a distinction is in the detail"*.

Time
"Time" not only refers to playing the correct rhythm, but also the correct tempo. Regarding rhythm, one aspect that many students miss is the lengths of notes. Most of the time, they will *start* the note in the correct place, but less often pay attention to when it finishes. This is especially so before rests.

The marking criteria also refers to *"rhythmic character well conveyed"*. Playing rhythms idiomatically adds character to a piece. For example, dotted rhythms can often become lazy, sounding almost like a triplet rhythm. On occasions is would be appropriate to use double dotting in early music, that is, a dotted quaver - semiquaver could be played as a double dotted quaver - demisemiquaver.

Similarly, in modern music, swing rhythms should not be allowed to become almost like dotted rhythms, but rather, have a more lazy, laid-back feel.

Regarding tempo, the ABRSM usually publishes a suggested metronome mark. However, this is **suggested, not obligatory.** Much more important is the **tempo mark** written by the composer. For example, *"Allegro",* doesn't just tell you how many crotchet beats per minute to play, but also tells you the **character** the composer intended, in this case *"lively".* Does your performance (including the tempo you choose), convey the character of the piece, that the composer had in mind? Don't get too hung up on metronome marks.

Added to this, music, like speaking, needs to breathe, have phrases, which sometimes includes easing off, or speeding up the tempo, the use of *rubato* becoming much more common in music from the Romantic period. Again, the marking criteria, awards a distinction for playing *"with flexibility where appropriate".*

Finally, within this assessment area, the examiner will be looking for fluency. As mentioned above, **a hesitation is a mistake.** Occasionally slips will happen, but try not to let them affect the flow of the music. Even professional musicians play wrong notes sometimes, but what you will never see them do is stop, go back, correct or hesitate in a performance.

Tone

For a distinction, the phrases used in the official marking criteria regarding tone include;

● Well projected

- Sensitive use of tonal qualities

Now the first area can have a lot to do with nerves. Many of us can tend to play very inwardly if we are not confident. However, consider this for a moment. A distinction is often awarded for a performance that includes a wrong note or two, but a distinction is rarely awarded for a *timid* performance where the student is so afraid of playing a wrong note that he plays too quietly or tentatively, thus missing the style and character of the piece.

Now, the quality of your tone depends on different things depending on what instrument you are playing, bowing / breathing technique for string and wind players, but for pianists and other instruments where playing one or more note simultaneously is possible, the examiner will be looking for one extra area, that is "*voicing*". This is when you give prominence to one particular part, the "voice", keeping accompanying parts softer and subservient. This is often, but not always, the upper part. So when you are preparing your piece, always be aware of where the melody is and give it a little extra weight. As mentioned above, listening to other *good* performances might be a useful tool in this regard.

Shaping

Music, like speaking, is divided into phrases and needs to breathe and for a distinction, the examiner will be looking for ***Expressive, idiomatic musical shaping and detail***. Here are some of the ways you can add shape to your playing

- Dynamics. - Phrases often tail off at the end of a phrase, or in the case of Baroque music, different phrases can be played with contrasting dynamic levels. Composers of earlier music, generally left interpretation of the dynamics to the performer and you will find that in many Baroque pieces in the ABRSM editions, no dynamics are written. This doesn't mean that you don't add any dynamic contrasts. On the contrary, the examiner will be looking for your interpretation, especially at the higher grades. On other occasions, dynamics in the part are *editorial* and a suggestion only. You should feel free to change what is written to your own interpretation and you will be given extra credit for creativity, as long as your performance is in keeping with the style and character of the piece. Just check that such dynamics (and sometimes articulation markings) are editorial and not the composer's own - there is usually a footnote at the end of the piece to say so, if this is the case.

● Articulation. - Pay attention to the phrase marks and legato/slur markings. At the end of a phrase, breathe, lift your bow or hand and even if you are not a wind player, think of the end of a phrase as a breath, where you would place a comma or full stop if it were spoken language. A similar concept is true for legato/slur markings. Always lift the last note of a slurred group. For example, if in a group of four quavers, the first three are slurred, make sure to slur onto the third note, which is then lifted. A common mistake is to lift the 2nd or 4th note.

● Changes is tempo. - Another way of adding shape to your playing is by sensitive changes of tempo. Depending on the period of music, you may want to let the tempo "ebb and flow" using *rubato* to add poignancy to certain moments. A sensitive use of rubato is the mark of a true musician (which is what the examiner is looking for to award you a distinction).

Again, listen to some good quality performances, listening out specifically for where changes in tempo are used. As I said, it will depend on the period of music and is more appropriate for music from the Romantic period onwards, but rubato can also be used to a lesser extent in Classical music and it would even be stylistic in many cases to *ritardando* at the end of a piece from the Baroque period.

Performance

Although the last area on the list of five we began with, it is probably the ***most important.*** Remember ***you are a musician, not a technician.*** Referring again to the official marking criteria, for a distinction, the examiner is looking for

- Assured
- Fully committed
- Vivid communication of character and style

Now, some of these areas will have overlap with others. For example, if you play *"assured and fully committed"* it will be projected with a confident tone. However, there is one word in the above list that I want to draw your attention to, which is - ***VIVID.*** One dictionary definition of the word vivid is, *"producing powerful feelings or strong, clear images in the mind"*. Does your performance do this???

One exercise I have used with my students, is to sketch or find and print out a drawing of what image the piece conveys. It could be a storm at sea, or some fairies dancing, whatever. Make it small enough that you can attach with a paper clip to the top of your music without obscuring the notes. Then before you play, look at this image and try portray this image through your performance.

A final word

Once you have learned your piece both musically and technically, you should be confident when going into the exam. Remember, one of the marking criteria for a distinction was "***Assured***". Go into the exam, believing in yourself, and when playing, you should have done enough preparation that you can even forget about the notes and ***ENJOY*** the performance. Yes that's right, I said "*enjoy*" in the context of an exam.

If you enjoy performing, the examiner will enjoy listening.

APPRASIAL SERVICE

There is no better boost to your confidence than knowing you are well prepared, which is why MusicOnline UK offer an appraisal service. This is like a mock exam before the real thing and takes place live via Skype.

Alternatively you might want a partial assessment of the individual aspects of the exam (maybe just one piece), by sending us video clips. In either case, you will get an appraisal of your performance including comments on where improvements can be made and an expected mark. I have many years of experience doing such "mock exams" with my own students, as well as online submissions and invariably my assessment is very close to the final mark received.

Details of this service can be found at:

https://www.music-online.org.uk/p/skype-lessons.html

Printed in Great Britain
by Amazon

80317925R00027